MOUNT LEBANON

MOUNT LEBANON

Poems

KARL KIRCHWEY

A MARIAN WOOD BOOK
Published by G. P. Putnam's Sons
a member of Penguin Group (USA) Inc.
New York

A MARIAN WOOD BOOK
Published by G. P. Putnam's Sons
Publishers Since 1838
a member of the Penguin Group
Penguin Group (USA) Inc., 375 Hudson Street, New York, New York 10014, USA •
Penguin Group (Canada), 90 Eglinton Avenue East, Suite 700, Toronto, Ontario M4P 2Y3,
Canada (a division of Pearson Penguin Canada Inc.) • Penguin Books Ltd, 80 Strand,
London WC2R 0RL, England • Penguin Ireland, 25 St Stephen's Green,
Dublin 2, Ireland (a division of Penguin Books Ltd) • Penguin Group
(Australia), 250 Camberwell Road, Camberwell, Victoria 3124, Australia
(a division of Pearson Australia Group Pty Ltd) • Penguin Books India Pvt Ltd,
11 Community Centre, Panchsheel Park, New Delhi–110 017, India •
Penguin Group (NZ), 67 Apollo Drive, Rosedale, North Shore 0632, New Zealand
(a division of Pearson New Zealand Ltd) • Penguin Books (South Africa) (Pty) Ltd,
24 Sturdee Avenue, Rosebank, Johannesburg 2196, South Africa

Penguin Books Ltd, Registered Offices: 80 Strand, London WC2R 0RL, England

Library of Congress Cataloging-in-Publication Data

Kirchwey, Karl, date.
Mount Lebanon : poems / Karl Kirchwey.
p.   cm.
ISBN 978-0-399-15727-1
1. Shakers—Poetry.   2. Mount Lebanon (N.Y.)—Poetry.   I. Title.
PS3561.I684M68   2011   2010039546
811'.54—dc22

Printed in the United States of America
1   3   5   7   9   10   8   6   4   2

BOOK DESIGN BY SUSAN WALSH

For Elinor, at last.

CONTENTS

. . .   This symbol is used to indicate a stanza break at the top or bottom of a page.

ACKNOWLEDGMENTS

Some of these poems have appeared in journals, to whose editors grateful acknowledgment is made:

Agni Review: "Barnegat Light," "A Wood Thrush"

The American Scholar: "Epigrams on the Fig," "Love in the Museum," "Sonnet," "Two Cardinals"

Arion: A Journal of the Humanities and the Classics: "Alaric and Romanus," "Blue," "Cheddar Pinks," "The Lake"

Harvard Divinity Bulletin: "A Dagger of Lath," "Faun's Head" (from the French of Arthur Rimbaud), "In the Garden (1)" (as "A Stone Buddha"), "Weeding"

The Hopkins Review: "A Cement Lawn Statue," "Why I Am Not a Musician"

Literary Imagination: "Ortho"

Little Star: "After Three Years" (from the French of Paul Verlaine)

The New Criterion: "Amicus," "Lenox Road" (as "Three Oaks")

The New Republic: "Gout-Weed" (as "A Cantata of Bach"), "July 20, 1969"

The New York Review of Books: "U.S. Route 20"

The New Yorker: "Propofol"

Parnassus: Poetry in Review: "Post Holes"
Poetry (Chicago): "ΛΗΜΝΟΣ," "The Red Portrait"
Salmagundi: "On a Pediment at Ta Prohm," "Siberian Iris,"
   "Viagra Nation"
Slate: "Wissahickon Schist"
Southwest Review: "September"
The Yale Review: "In the Garden (2)," "Late Figs"

"Belfagor" appeared in *Alhambra Poetry Calendar 2009: 366
Classic and Contemporary Poems;* "Fine Work with Pitch and
Copper" appeared in *Alhambra Poetry Calendar 2008.*

"After Three Years" is included in my complete translation of
Paul Verlaine's *Poèmes saturniens* (*Poems Under Saturn*),
published by Princeton University Press.

The epigraphs to sections I and II are taken from *Visiting the
Shakers, 1778–1849,* edited by Glendyne R. Wergland and
published by Richard W. Couper Press (2007). My thanks to
editor Randy Ericson and to Glendyne Wergland for permission
to quote the accounts in this book.

To Tamzen Flanders and to Marian Wood, as always, infinite
thanks; and to Kate Davis and Anna Jardine.

I. SPIRIT-LAND

Perhaps nature never formed a more appropriate spot for the
dwelling of a sober, enlightened, and a religious people. . . .
There is throughout the whole scene, a striking conformity of
art to nature. You are here presented with no object which
excites a painful admiration by its vastness and sterility, but
every thing within the vision of the spectator, conveys assurance
of its adaptation to some important and useful purpose.

—ANONYMOUS VISITOR, *describing the Shaker community*
at New Lebanon, New York (1817)

NEW GULPH ROAD

Krishna says, *I am the pure fragrance
that comes from the earth,
and the brightness of fire I am.*

What was it you meant to say?

Something about this March day,
the beech leaves' trembling pallor
in low places past the rhododendron's
curl and glaze; the schist's covert glitter,
requiring words and beyond them;

something in all of this that pardons
the effort and its failure both.

WISSAHICKON SCHIST

What did you think the color of learning was,
if not mica and hornblende flashing in a long-settled gray?

You look for a plane along which it will cleave
to admit the self, but it is you who are divided

always between resolution and doubt,
having read *A small amount of fissile material*

was smuggled across, remembering certain islands
long ago, the windblown passages between,

wild thyme on the offshore breeze from Lemnos,
or the white slash of a coral runway at Tinian.

You open a book to the stories of changing forms
and see the guts of a mole exploded on the lawn,

a red-tailed hawk balanced nonchalant on the railing,
and the day's light cut on such a deep bias,

· · ·

one February afternoon, with a thousand starlings
aligned in the branches of the silver pendant linden,

that it seems the whole earth will tip into a chasm of dark.
You write *A secret lapis, shedding* . . . then stop.

Into what? The iridescent chatter of those birds,
the shoulder of the wind, any horizontal thing.

Alone in the silence, you write . . . *into crystalline shells,*
as the walls rise up around you with their faint glitter.

A WOOD THRUSH

A wood thrush flew
into the picture window
of my friend's house upstate
and broke its neck
and lay broken
on the hardwood deck,
both that which had its end
and that which did not
because it was reflected:

so from the dark adjournment
of his flat screen,
my friend decided
to conjure the bird back,
unclench the tarses, spread
the wings which had been folded
in the economy of death.
Again the whisker mark
led to the freckled breast;

he summoned all the rest,
and taught the mandibles to part,

that song itself might start
out of a silence
deeper than before—
except that he had never
heard the thrush sing,
had not been fetched
the offhand blow

of recollected sweetness,
recollected woe,
had never waited,
sick with listening,
and thought, *How does it go?*
My visual ingenious friend
restored a bird
he had not heard
and did not know.

BELFAGOR

Summers, facing east
at my window in the forest,
I watch light splash and freckle

crotch and stem and leaf-blade,
the badge and scar of it
trembling in the breeze.

Belfagor, Pan, Dionysus,
will you not come
and stand in that sun-warm

blazon of leaf mold
where always I expect you?
Will you not step forth

out of the teasing shadow,
resolve yourself at last
from light into matter?

．　．　．

Now I am gray with waiting,
like the ancient mask
of the doe's face

I saw turn toward me
at the forest's edge
in the perfect stillness,

ears and scut erect,
and her two fawns with her,
not in a sensual train

like something out of Bouguereau
with shrieking pipe and timbrel,
but simply vanishing

with the thrush's song
re-echoing from somewhere
deeper in the forest.

Will you not relent?
I call you once more: Come.
I will not last forever.

MOUNT LEBANON

Passed to Immortality.

—*Shaker grave marker*

I came to this place as I had done before,
  first tasting the blessèd water of the spring,
    because a stillness in me needed testing
      against more than the rumor of the world.
So I drove up from the valley's pig manure
    and dirt-track speedway to the ancient seed-bed

of radical truths—but found it somehow *less*,
  become mere factories or human hives,
    lodgments for such fiercely circumscribed lives,
      whose windows, set in row on empty row,
I had admired for light and loveliness
      seemed purely repetitious to me, though

their Elder, after all, had warned that "beauty,
    absurd and abnormal, has no business with us"
      (the sky-blue ceiling of the meeting house,
        slim shank of a chair or curve of a box)
"as long as people live in misery."
      It angered me, such willful paradox:

. . .

that male and female might, loving, subsist

as one in God, yet be denied the work

of natural generation, for the spark

of earthly love, what they called "fleshing off,"

they impatiently, contemptuously dismissed.

Beside their great burned stone barn in my self

I burned for these, by their own paradigm

strictly extinct, the obscure forest plot

to which their congress with the world of spirit

led them at last. And how could it surprise,

when I was summoned from my broken dream

by a regretful and insistent voice

belonging, not to their Mother Ann Lee,

but the headmistress of the boarding school

the place was now? I fit some vagrant's profile,

challenged to state my business, where a Coke can

propped a listening casement, as she told me

this place was private and I must move on.

U.S. ROUTE 20

Past Kinderhook, where she swam as a child,
    shadowed now and overhung with branches,
so that it is invisible from the road,
    ahead of you, an August cloudscape is

massing in ramparts over Lebanon Valley
    and the mountain Shakers called "the back side of
this world, connecting with eternity."
    But they are long gone, hands, hearts, work, and love,

and there is no one at the Valley Rest Motel.
    William J. Culhane Used Cars has a Subaru
you ought to look at, but you never will,
    and there's a tractor-trailer rig for sale too,

high windshield dazzling, too bright to bear,
    wide wings to lift and carry you away
with a full plate of ICC tags (but to where?)
    on roads bordered by Queen Anne's lace and chicory

and, at the foot of a billboard, loosestrife.
    Tobacco, teen pregnancy, drunk driving,

an alpine water slide, I BEAT MY WIFE . . .
  AT BACKGAMMON. If you reach Ward Hatch Plumbing,

you've gone too far. For did you not, just as
  your heart began to drag with the familiar
torn love for everything you know will pass,
  see, on your right, a field of purple heather

empty and radiant in the afternoon,
  and on your left, in plain caps without irony
outside the Church of the Immaculate Conception,
  the legend MY WORDS WILL NOT PASS AWAY?

ALARIC AND ROMANUS

If everything you have written
is forgotten at your death,
just a waste of breath,
the labor of putting words in order,
of listening, trying to remember,

then you will be like Alaric,
the Visigoth king, who died
in 410 at Cosenza,
but not before he had commanded
that the Busento River

be diverted from its course
and he with all his treasure
buried under the gravel,
so when it returned to its bed,
clouded with the blood

of the slaves who had buried him,
no one alive could say where,
under the braided currents,

the one who had sacked Rome
after eleven hundred years lay;

or like the Byzantine emperor
Romanus Lecapenus,
banished by his own sons
to the prison island of Prote,
who on Holy Thursday in 946,

saved by the Virgin Mary,
before an audience of three hundred
read his sins aloud from the book
in which he had written them,
and sent it to a holy monk

named Dermocaetes on Mount Olympus
who fasted and prayed for his soul
until one night a voice cried out three times,
"God's mercy has conquered!"
and all the pages were blank.

AMICUS

These mornings, I wake feeling as if, during the night,
    I had been tried by a jury of my peers
    and found—*But wait, fellow citizens! Fifty-two years*
and no appeal? Is there no merciful alternate?

All those I have loved come by in a long parade,
    their faces strangely tender, etched and grave
    with my own lost intent and their belief.
Through half-closed eyelids I see those who have died,

glaring or bashful in the little tea-lights of my sleep.
    Oaring the thick medium time, they seem to yaw
    toward me in a sort of pregnant slo-mo,
but I can never read their straining lips,

and when dawn strands me in its courthouse square,
    my body heavy in the deceitful sun,
    my sentence to get through the day again,
they retire once more charged to their muffled chamber.

THREE DREAMS

1. The Red Portrait

Last night she came to me, my mother, dead,
but as she was in the photo, that last Christmas,
wearing a red dress, and her lipstick was red
(I wonder if that means she lives in hell),
and I saw again that she was beautiful,
the same high forehead I have, the same wide brow,
and my age, forty-nine; and now I was
talking fast, because I knew I had no time,
and I told her I loved her, I told her how her life
had informed mine, and I begged her to come
to me again, to meet my children, my wife.
I said to her— My work, see what I have made,
I have tried to do what you did not live to do.
But she smiled at me and began to fade.

2. Another Dream of the Master

Who are you? You are what I do not know,
felt as imperative. Now speak to me.

You are idea, silence and shadow.
Why should you come to me more frequently

than my own father, dead these twenty years?
Nothing of which I am capable is proof;
no labor of mine ever satisfies.
I think you are uncompromising love.

Your confidential eye, your hurrying voice,
your fierce opinion scalding me to think,
knowledge being mortal and words never careless:
I have learned. Master, will you never speak,

having set in me this constant hunger?
Always, always it happens this way,
obedient to some remorseless order:
I wake before I can hear what you say.

3. The Lake

In my dream, the Lake opened westward
toward the city where my mother died,
and I (who once would have been quick

to worship it) heard a voice speak,
her voice, but also Creusa's, and say,
as on the last night of burning Troy,
   You have fled from me Iulus

as though she had brought me to that height
to show me a world I did not know yet,
its cities lovely, its ample countries,
she who has been in eternity thirty years
(to speak of time where there is no time,
neither in death nor in dream):
   You have fled from me Iulus

Moon-silvered and reluctant,
the Lake crawled by, far below, silent,
the lapped beauty of each wave
like a debt she would never forgive,
the fact of my life as I stood.
She opened her knees; I was made.
   You have fled from me Iulus

And I spoke out at last and said Yes
(I knew I had to answer that voice),
Creusa Mother Darling Precious Queen,

The place where you died was not my own.
My father led me into the west:
all night we flew, after you were lost.

You have fled from me Iulus

Will you not release me from this dream?
At my back, then, I felt the dawn come,
the Lake raddled with salmon and coral,
and that wandering voice never still,
unappeasable, rising, because
she had loved me before I ever was:

You have fled from me Iulus

McGRATH ROAD

The house shrugs back gradually into the hillside,
    and a single book sprawls open in the dust.
First two maiden brothers farmed here. When they died,
    a woman lawyer bought it for a lovenest

and moved across the road into the stable.
    She lived alone for years with her TV.
From there on winter nights would leap and fall
    the blue glow of elliptical narrative,

like this page from the *New York Supplement* (Second Series):
    "One evening in November, 1932 . . ."
The rest has passed through the gut of a chipmunk or a field mouse,
    lost in the phlox, nettles and false mallow.

LENOX ROAD

I stopped this morning on a curve of the Lenox Road,
just where East Road branches off (you won't know where
    this is,
I realize), because of a—a feeling of accomplished peace,
I guess I'd call it, though such a phrase can't be trusted.
What I mean to say is that, often before, I had been tempted,
driving past, to stop at that grove of three oak trees,
where a barred gate and some fence posts' staggered silvers
contained a hillside pasture still unmowed
even in mid-July: and this time I *did* stop.
That's it, really. Nothing at all changed, in the deep
shadows of those trees or the several boulders
left to wait in that field by the last glaciers;
and the silence relied on no answer from anything human.
So I got back in my car and I drove on.

SINISTER

When at last the dark shape
slews across the double yellow line,
coming on at fifty-five or sixty
downhill through the steep
double S-curve,
looking for *you* unmistakably,
with no chance to dodge and weave
or outwit the grand design

in this case executed
by a late-model SUV
(a prestige import, no less),
you might do well to be flattered,
and conquer the resistance
of whatever in you deplores
such randomness, the prudence
of nearly a lifetime, suddenly

finding yourself, with a clash of the cymbal,
ushered into a cunning labyrinth
of pleated linen drapes and cut glass,
the zip code exclusive, but not your style.

Nor is it the addled one,

drunk at the wheel, who spatters

Mollydooker Red across fawn

upholstery (vineyard of the Enchanted Path),

who will remain in memory.

There is someone else to thank

for this tangent, in its pure

ruthlessness—not the one who drove away,

after a single moment of

usefulness; not the name on the blotter,

but someone who almost had your life:

and you know her. Her name is _____.

II. FLESHING OFF

But—where is the warrant, either in reason or in scripture, by which whole communities, (not here and there, individuals, peculiarly situated,) withdraw themselves from the most interesting and important of social relations—from the tender charities of husband and wife—from the delightful assiduities of parental love—from that relation, on which society stands, and on which as on a fruitful stock, is grafted, every personal and domestic virtue, and every hope, both for this world and a better!

—BENJAMIN SILLIMAN, *describing the Shaker community at New Lebanon, New York (1819)*

PROPOFOL

Moly, mandragora, milk of oblivion:
    I said to Doctor Day, "You bring on night."
"But then," he said, "I bring day back again,"
    and smiled; except his smile was thin and slight.

I said to him, "Sleep and Death were brothers,
    you know. They carry off great Troy's Sarpedon
in Euphronios' famous calyx-krater"
    —babbling. He said, "I am a singleton."

I said to him, "The Romans would have called you
    Somnus, the Greeks Hypnos or Morpheus"
(but Doctor Day looked blank), anything to
    forestall the wasp (Classics not his thing, I guess)

alighting on the back of my right hand.
    He said to me, "Tell me why you are here."
I said, "To lose a page, I understand,
    out of the Book of Life." A traveler

.   .   .

approached the citadel even while I was speaking,

    seven seconds from my brain: then it was snuff.

Pornokrates, naked in her black stocking,

    led one more pig on a leash to the trough.

ORTHO

Sunlight prinks this trash,
    flotsam thrown from a Yukon
by now too far away to reach
    with the rumor of getting it on.

In a landscape sown with salt,
    pledges of life remain.
Item: a crocus-colored foil packet,
    or the delicate torn saffron

that wrapped the ingenious small wheel,
    so brazen where it lies,
each blue or white or green pill
    through the lengthening days,

though perhaps it was instead
    night that stirred the hunger
to scatter these on the road:
    let it be darker, longer,

. . .

let it fully inhabit

    the touch of body and body,
the final extinction of it,

    like the drowning of an army.

Both ironic and chaste,

    the sow's purse of the spring
proclaims the winter lost:

    these are the tokens of its vanishing.

Rain winks on a packet of foil.

    How fresh, how sweet and clean!
Beyond the clouded crystal,

    a savor that is barren.

Poor wrinkled bud, poor callus-

    colored O, how will you
people the world? Pale narcissus,

    tell me how you will grow

in a bed of sand. Profligate,

    do these proofs of the eye
offend you? Pluck them out:

    they will come back perpetually.

ΛΗΜΝΟΣ

the deep male growl of the sea-lashed headland

—*Philoctetes*

August long ago, the summer Lemnian
(not like the deeds of those who killed their men),
the self a glowing bead, like Hephaestus falling
daylong out of heaven in the old story,
the island's interior a forge, a glory-hole,
the odor of wild thyme borne offshore steadily,
the Aegean Sea purple, wine-dark, without epithet;
and as I walked on the beach, my mother not long dead,
the perfect crystal of my self-regard
so lately flawed, and landscape made to echo
my own low cry in the island's empty places,
I found a pure white bone that wind and salt
had scoured of every grief and all self-pity:
and so I came to the love of others.

SONNET

Tell me something I don't know about love.

The story goes that Paul Verlaine's mother,
Élisa-Julie-Josèphe-Stéphanie Dehée,
kept her miscarried fetuses in a jar.
The poet, returning home drunk one night,
smashed them on the stone dining room floor.

Tell me something else.

Casanova once loved a woman who did not love him.
So he collected bits of her hair,
had them made into candies, and ate them secretly.

Love must not touch the marrow of the soul.

A poet said that, a long time ago.

Our affections must be breakable chains.

Snail-track of jism? No, that was the moon,
    silvering the tongue-and-groove of floor,
    my parents arguing outside on the stair,
the primal "We should get a divorce" scene

(sound up and over: from *The Guiding Light*).
    I slept. I woke. And there in the TV's
    old one-eye, pallid figures up to the knees
in last winter's wood ashes, utter night,

dark as whatever I could put my mind to,
    twinkling overhead, while Father Frost
    guarded the empty hearth and Madame Triste
slung firewater as she was wont to do,

their voices faint with joy or just with distance.
    And so from history I birthed myself,
    beyond the orbits of these two whom love
prevented from admitting my existence.

. . .

I crossed a threshold in my body somewhere,
I felt it, and there was no going back.
Lie still, I said, and coast the roaring dark.
Light fled in its frail line beneath the door.

VILLANELLE ON TWO LINES
BY MARK STRAND

The mind is honest but the body lies.
You cannot know the person who was meant.
I am myself; I am my own disguise:

no greater misery beneath the skies,
surely, no more deceptive ornament.
The mind is honest but the body lies,

a kind of mask to mistranslate my cries,
this body, luminous and palpitant.
I am myself; I am my own disguise.

Some order would not have it otherwise:
body hides mind; the sinner hides the saint.
The mind is honest but the body lies

in its stale sheets, its little paradise
of tangled limbs, its spliff and blandishment.
I am myself; I am my own disguise,

·   ·   ·

beyond all power to alter or revise
or recover original intent.
The mind is honest but the body lies.
I am myself; I am my own disguise.

WHY I AM NOT A MUSICIAN

for William Logan

In the decently opulent lobby
of the Curtis Institute of Music,
I waited to meet a friend for lunch.

Amid the dark wood paneling
and hot radiators, under the gaze
of a young woman in an oil painting

with wings growing out of her back,
I listened with a vague contentment
that did not need to be more specific

to a quartet rehearsing Brahms somewhere,
brass working a section of *Carmen*
and, not two weeks before Christmas,

continuo passages from *Messiah*:
all the promiscuous beautiful cross-talk
musicians are so good at,

•   •   •

meaning nothing, addressed to no one.
And I found myself remembering
how once, at the age of nineteen,

with no previous musical training,
I decided to become a violist.
I appeared before those who had devoted

their lives to its strict discipline
with my cheap student instrument in a case
I had chosen, for some reason, to carry

in the monogrammed laundry bag
I once had at summer camp.
No, I know why I did that: because

the instrument seemed too beautiful to touch,
though my girlfriend, who was a musician,
was not too beautiful to touch.

And what I remembered best of all
was the savage amusement of the master
and everyone in his studio

. . .

at this holy fool who was wearing

his own initials like a doom

for everyone to see, and who had so completely

misunderstood the nature of what is beautiful

that he thought it could be written out in words.

A flush of shame made me look at my watch

and discover I had been waiting an hour.

No sign of my friend, so I nodded

to Euterpe and went out for a sandwich.

ALBA

A rift of crimson

          in the east

the groin of a girl

          from long ago

her straight back rising

          from the bed

like the flank

          of a sycamore

beyond the window

          She was on the phone

negotiating

          her escape

I watched the future

          come undone

but had eyes only

          for the dark place

where the leaves gathered

          pale so pale

in an angle of stone

          To talk, to touch

even to smile

          these were beyond me

Day when it came

                was level and cold

and owed me nothing

                  That blinding tree

they cut it down

LOVE IN THE MUSEUM
(Merion, Pennsylvania)

Love is not like Renoir.
This you might have said
as we lay on your bed
later, our bodies not touching.

The easy fall of hair,
the volumes of flesh stippled,
the underwater light,
the women violet-eyed.

I can still hear your voice:
No, love is like the whore
painted by van Gogh.
Love is the gravity

that distorts her bare breast,
the way she can't inhabit
the rectangular canvas
that he tears to an oval.

. . .

Love is like the woman
seen from below
in the painting by Courbet
as she lies on her back

and pulls on one stocking,
her pallid body
indifferent and open.
Love, even in Renoir,

is like the alizarin
strokes by which a figure
is both highlight and shadow
of its own mortality.

And then? What happened then,
that winter afternoon,
as the light failed around us?
Or perhaps you said nothing.

LIBERTY ICE CREAM PARLOR

Spring drove the green fuse that year through Charles Street.
    We slept together at your aunt's, remember?
But she kept cats. My eyes swelled nearly shut:
    blindness of histamines. Love made me blinder.

You limped a little from the accident
    in Paris still. I loved your dark blond hair;
your crooked leg; your pea-green winter coat;
    your laugh (a downward scale in G minor);

your fingers when you put them to your flute;
    your eyelids, livid as storm, veined and tender;
all love's anatomy: why mention it,
    when most of all I loved my own rapture?

How could one feel so deeply and be so ignorant?
    We rode uptown to the Liberty Ice Cream Parlor
after embraces tantric in their heat,
    and fed your considerable sweet tooth there,

· · ·

under a copy of Bartholdy's statue.

 I heard the place had been demolished last year,

but as I hurried west in the noon's racket,

  I ran into you, quite by chance, just where

we once thought life conspired for our delight.

 Brief exclamations of surprise and pleasure;

a lingering. The rest wasn't difficult,

  photos of children, date-books, promises (later

we would call each other, but we didn't).

 I looked up and saw building-wrap shiver

in the March sky. Steel teetered at the balance point,

  and something else for a moment swung higher,

a shadow threatening to crush me flat

 beneath it, a helplessness both familiar

and more than thirty years forgotten, so that

  it seemed a kind of mercy brought me where,

finding myself released into a sunlit

 avenue toward the end of winter,

I turned, wanting to tell you of it, but

  found we had parted sometime earlier.

FINE WORK WITH PITCH AND COPPER

A girl stands by the rounded silver flank
of the BMW in which her lover waits,
gray-haired, thick-waisted. Or maybe it's her father.
She wears a sleeveless top in February,
as if she would outface the shadow-casts
of the low sun falling on her belly and breasts.
Across the dead landscape comes the clatter
of roofers' hammers on a gray stone house.
They are working mirror-lengths of clean new copper
and shaving wood shingles so they fit close
against the imminent return of weather.
The girl stands like forsythia lured into bloom
then struck with frost. The roofers look beyond her,
at the heartless beauty of the flank of the car.

VIAGRA NATION

E-mails from Chastity Rutland or Valorie Breedlove
    wait in my in-box like tumescence in the morning,
or like the breakfast tabloid headlines of
    the deceived wife who attacked her husband, sleeping

so blandly beside her, and ripped out his joystick
    (as teenagers they had taken the abstinence pledge).
They attend my waking like the little music
    of small birds fussing prettily in the hedge,

promising "steel-hard erections," orgasms "longer
    and more intense than any you've ever known,"
ejaculations (as to volume? force?) "like a porn star,"
    and increases in length just short of serpentine:

so that I think of Tiresias, the amazed thump
    of his staff across those snakes coupling in a glade,
who felt the gap in his own being damp
    with longing to imagine the other side;

· · ·

again the fir-top whispers as King Pentheus
    rides it into the sky to spy on love,
dazed, clinging, eager in a woman's dress,
    before his own mother tears his head off.

A GLASS OF WATER

My daughter, twelve,
    canters into morning,
    in her place leaving
the latest fiction to involve

a girl just like her
    (but more richly gowned,
    more superbly threatened)
and a glass of water

standing half full on
    the butter-yellow oilcloth,
    something to play with
the early sun,

as prismatic gouts
    go burning and reeling
    across the ceiling;
as if my thoughts

were a carousel as random,
    allowing me

to find, in the water's clarity,
her soul's best emblem,

not as a thing apart,
    either, from the captive
    heartfelt narrative,
that moment's indigo or violet

in which I notice
    my pulse, through the table,
    make a surface tremble
that would be still otherwise.

BARNEGAT LIGHT

One day we climbed the slim bicolored lighthouse
    to admire the view,
up the 217 yellow-painted stairs,
    give or take a few.

We paused to read about the useful sneak-box,
    the plover's spotted eggs,
and littoral transport, a kind of liminal crux.
    "I'm afraid in my legs,"

my daughter said on the way down. At the bottom,
    past the wrinkled rose, a pair
of sleeping owl-faced binoculars in chrome
    blinked awake for half a dollar.

I asked her to tell me everything she saw.
    "A sunburned angry man,"
she said, "who's just asked for a piña colada
    from someone named John."

Then a park ranger nearby misspoke himself.
    He said the snipers weren't running

(by which he meant stripers). We didn't laugh
at the inadvertent cunning

of his remark, though, but felt it in the silence:
the tower *was* vulnerable,
and we were being sieved by circumstance.
We made a loose circle:

"For the next twenty years, this country will be at war,
and I'd like to see
how we go about making that fact square
with our precious democracy."

Suddenly I came down from some high place,
past slippers made of felt
left at the door to keep the pristine lenses
from every beam or mote;

and there was no wisdom, foolishness only,
for seven gallons of oil,
integrity spent, grain by grain, to justify
the merely plausible.

*   *   *

A crack in the breakwater seemed to widen
between neighbor and friend
at such a rate it risked becoming soon
too deep ever to mend,

and ancient darkness lifted its thick muzzle,
poised to close from the east
upon the faltering torch once visible
thirty miles at least.

BLUE

So he comes home one day, his hair dyed blue,
  and for a moment all the world is stilled
before the prodigy. Vision is dazed, too,
   by this cyanic swath, this chunk of sky felled,

ticklish, in anger or in whimsy—not like
  surprising rinses you have sometimes seen
in stifling rooms, adoze over the clink
   of mah-jongg tiles or what's up on the screen.

You take a breath and start to speak—but don't.
  That's good. For sure, it's unaccountable,
but thank God not (yet) a tattoo. It isn't
   body piercing, something more irreversible,

tongue stud or nose ring or the pinna of the ear
  armored with tiny hoops. It could be worse.
Think of . . . what was her name? Scylla, the teenager
   in one of Ovid's *Metamorphoses,*

who falls in love with Minos, king of Crete,
  besieging her city, and who decides

to visit her father while he sleeps and cut
off the scalplock where his strength resides.

She offers it to Minos, who refuses,
but still the city falls. She is changed to
a shearwater, but not before she says,
"He is the source of all my fear and sorrow"

—meaning her father. Count yourself lucky:
he still talks to you. You are still admired.
Are you blue? You begin and end that way.
Just give it time. Over time it will fade.

SEPTEMBER

Valley Forge: a last picnic at sunset.
    We are the four corners of the known world.
Briefly we stretch and touch on an old blanket:
    father, mother, child, and younger child.

The empty fields will soon go starveling
    around that stone house and its whitewashed wall.
Beyond the smell of summer dust is something
    later, drier, more corruptible:

and yet it is slowly, reluctantly,
    we find our way across the crumbling dark,
vision dilated as the orderly
    headlights stream westward and out of the park,

until the only things with light left in them
    are tufts of milkweed in their blackened pods,
each twisted, burst, split open on its stem
    around a sky-soaked filament, a luminous floss.

III. IN THE GARDEN

IN THE GARDEN (1)

Buddha's almost gone in gout-weed.
His left hand's withered in his lap;

his right hand's raised in the *abhayamudra,*
the gesture for dispelling fear.

I turn fifty this year,
with only the callus on my left hand,

and the gods I have lived with, and those I love.
Decently out of his line of vision,

Aphrodite covers her breasts.
A slight breeze moves through the epicene fingers

of fig leaves smelling of sweat and sweetness.
A goldfinch teetering on a wire,

.   .   .

thorn-eater, symbol of the Resurrection,
flies off on a long undulation.

And then a sudden burst of rain
shakes the fifteen umbels of Buddha.

A DAGGER OF LATH

Here is a dagger of lath
hewn from a limb of white pine,
bleeding and resinous.

I found it, a poignard lashed
with common garden twine,
in the chevelure of lawn

where he must have dropped it
after the feint, slash and spin
of imaginary combat.

But where is the tiger of wrath
that waits in everything human?
I have seen that stalk him too,

perplex his feet, cloud his eye,
the mirthless cruelty
that weeps at its own devices.

. . .

Quick, I will hide it again,
that he might not fall on its blade,
my first-born, my slender one.

AFTER THREE YEARS

Having pushed open the narrow wobbling gate,
I strolled around in the little garden
Gently illuminated by the morning sun
Spangling each flower with a damp flash of light.

The simple arbor: it's all still here, nothing's different,
The madly growing vines, the chairs of cane . . .
Always making its silver murmur, the fountain,
And the old aspen its perpetual lament.

Just as before, the roses throb; as before,
The huge proud lilies waver in the air.
I know every lark, coming and going.

I've even found the statue of the barbarian prophetess
Still upright down the walk, her plaster spalling,
—Slender, amid the mignonette's insipidities.

—from the French of Paul Verlaine (1844–1896)

GOUT-WEED

When I had grappled for hours with ground elder,
        trefoil, umbel-flowered, its stem touched crimson,
its roots multiplied beyond measure;

when tendrils of wisteria I had seen
        tentative at morning in a single day
leapt a void of air, conniving, stubborn;

when I had seen the bruised carnal profligacy
        of shattered wine- and cream-colored petals
arrayed around the stem of the peony;

when I had also known the mortal smells
        of intimacy cradled by the fig
daylong in its green shade and blunt dactyls,

then I turned to where you listened to *Christ lag*
        in Todesbanden, the shadows at your eyes,
across your lap a bright crocheted rug,

and knew by what the garden would outlast us.

SIBERIAN IRIS

No words for certain colors—coreopsis,
    lychnis, Siberian iris, the garden in June—
    in their ransomed intensity, I mean;
except, unbidden, there arises this
    memory of the island of Saipan:

the western shore, Susupe, Green Beach Two,
    and still in the lagoon where it had foundered
    driving for shore, its cannon raised, angled
against hills hostile sixty Junes ago,
    a rusting Sherman tank, toward which I waded,

through crystalline shallows, then briefly swam,
    drawn by its strangeness, its incongruity.
    The tranquil waters of the Philippine Sea
polarized the sunlight into random
    flares of pure neon, as it seemed to me,

touching, warmly rinsing the empty hull,
    sluicing freely through the open hatches,
    transparent except for a few coughs and catches

around the ancient steel burled thick with coral,
   a sacrament perpetual and monotonous,

far from the original smoke, blood and filth
   that had prevailed. I put my face in the water
   and saw, at ease around the ancient armor,
fish brilliant as these flowers in their earth,
   as if tricked by the eye out of grim war.

FIREFLIES

Vers les buissons errent les lucioles . . .
    but that was another language, another time.
    Better say they thread the gout-weed's crimson stem,
flat-hatting through the lychnis, and then stall

deep in the fig; or, like the London–Dallas
    nonstop, they drift by, blinking overhead,
    long for pale Aphrodite, err toward
her crossed arms, her budded areolas

pale in the dusk, illuminated greenly
    in that style called *Venus Italica,*
    or ornament the tendrils of wisteria
and ground-loop in the compost, signaling feebly

from (it may be) a lettuce leaf, so drenched,
    so gilded with Italic extra-virgin
    that, although restored to the darkening lawn,
they cannot rise, and are like tapers quenched.

EPIGRAMS ON THE FIG

1.

On the island of Lemnos, where he fell,

I remember the figs were watered with liquid nightsoil.

2.

In the garden, when he walked in the cool of the day,

they heard his voice and hid behind a fig tree.

3.

He cursed the fig when he passed it the first time,

because he was hungry and it bore nothing for him.

4.

When he snared them in a net, they were making the fig,

Aphrodite and Ares, god of war, god of rage.

5.

From morn (according to the narrative)

to noon he fell, from noon to dewy eve.

.   .   .

6.

He devised a race of golden mechanical women
and placed a ripe fig at the center of each one.

7.

The island women decided to slaughter their husbands.
Blood splashed the fig leaves in fingered medallions.

8.

That basket of figs was also Cleopatra's,
joy of the worm and *Yare, yare, good Iras.*

9.

Or: *he stretched to pick a fig for my mother;*
an abscess burst; and he died in a few hours.

10.

And the island long ago when they woke to leave it:
dawn, like a fresh fig, was rimmed with scarlet.

WEEDING

Lawlessly they embroider
the mossed interstices

of every fixed pattern, and
stubbornly, too, whether

mouse-eared chickweed, yarrow or
broad-leafed plantain, until

the shortest way with them is
to dig the bricks out of

their bed of sand with a forked
tool, strip away the blind

and pulpy mesh of roots, then
resettle them snugly,

so they rub grainy shoulders
with a kind of music

. . .

like that you have heard breathing
through a terra-cotta

wind chime. What is surprising,
though, is how the day's warmth

lingers in the white sand, in
each long glazed flank of brick,

even after the sun is
gone, as if the real life

were elsewhere all the time, with
the roots that knew to thrive

away from the light, and you
no closer to knowledge

though having knocked the axis
of the world out of true,

standing in the disordered
garden with night coming on.

IN THE GARDEN (2)

So at last it ends,
a week of sweltering weather.
Dinner with our friends

on the patio,
and in the gathering dusk,
arcs of glittering water

as children prance and slither
across the lawn.
One child trains the hose

on my eleven-year-old daughter
as she careens toward me,
her body steeply angled

against gravity,
her hair a single fall,
and the look on her face—

.   .   .

Goldfinches carom off
through the wisteria arbor
in a triune epiphany;

fireflies startle up,
fleeing like rounds of tracer
in movies I have seen,

and in the moment's space
her joy should occupy,
what comes to mind instead

is a photograph
in which a naked girl,
her clothes burned off by napalm,

runs down a country road,
GIs walking behind her.
I cannot hear her scream.

ON A PEDIMENT AT TA PROHM

What the regime taught was renunciation,
and anyone, it seemed, who could not learn
to make a basketball court into a vegetable garden
was killed with a pickaxe, a cudgel, or a helve.
Most particularly forbidden was ordinary love
between husband and wife, or parents and children.

If you thread the stone-gray roots of the silk cotton
and teeter on a pile of rubble, there will open
before you, its figures vivid and moss-green
in their multiplied geometry, a bas-relief
of the night Siddhartha Gautama left his wife,
whose name was Yasodhara, and his son,

whose name was Rahula. He gazed at the palace women
as they slept, their careless bodies so soon
to be extinct, content with being human,
warm and splayed with nothing more than life;
and kneeling gods with their palms muffled the hooves of
his horse, none waking from their concussion.

FAUN'S HEAD

In the jewel-box maculate with gold, in the greenness,
In the uncertain greenness flourishing
With splendid flowers where the kiss dozes,
Alive in the exquisite embroidery he is tearing,

He shows his two eyes, a scared faun,
And bites the red flowers with his white teeth.
Burnished and bloody like an old wine,
His lip breaks into laughter in the undergrowth,

And when—like a squirrel—he has fled,
His laugh still trembles on each leaf,
And the golden kiss of the woods, startled
By a bullfinch, you can see commune with itself.

—from the French of Arthur Rimbaud (1854–1891)

CHEDDAR PINKS

(after Robert Bridges)

I bought a big terra-
 cotta pot with a
chaste meander running
 round the edge, and set
it on the broken brick
 patio, and sat
reading the *Odyssey*
 in a modern trans-
lation, but those flowers
 mocked me in silence,
really more like something
 out of Dr. Seuss,
dauphin-crimson velvet
 with paired comic spots,
white, on each petal: prim,
 high-necked, rising from
gray stalks with just a faint
 smell of cinnamon,
like Mary Poppins' face,
 come to think of it,

in the illustrations

    by Mary Shepard;

so that for all I might

    bend the world to the

pot's rim, teach narrative

    to circle home at

last, in the breathless heat

    of noon, these motley

flowers burned on with a

    defiant whimsy,

their courage ludicrous,

    as if to assert

(but rightly) that nothing

    more demure than these

is worth remembering.

A CEMENT LAWN STATUE

Once I caught her full in the face with Roundup.
Little sparrows, lecherous in the bushes,
hushed their brawls; doves, too, quit their endless mourning,
    watched me and waited,

for it seemed to me that her nipples stiffened,
roused to indignation. The checkered shadow
dazed me. White and smooth, her flank told me nothing,
    but I was fearful,

praying, *Foam-Born, Goddess, I've served you, faithful,*
Aphrodite, how many years? You know it.
Pity me this culpable fervor, Cypris!
    Only remember

how much else I've spared from the cankering poison,
all I could, the mutable and the holy.
Why should one, though, flourish above all others?
    Rather, should not a

· · ·

balance still prevail in your lovely precincts?
If I raise this wand to proliferating
nature, it is never without the knowledge
      I, too, will wither.

Then, as bishop's weed with its lace-white flowers
shook beneath the mist from my hand-pumped sprayer,
sun made rainbows through it like eros' wingbeats.
      I was forgiven.

POST HOLES

I have been replacing fence posts this summer—
    not, I think, out of any particular need
    to enclose that which is mine (for indeed
my demesne in this world is quite minor),

nor because good fences make good neighbors (they do,
    but my neighbor is more competent than I),
    nor because the old ones are rotten, though they are, surely,
but because the earth feels more familiar the deeper I go,

in its crumbled alternating veins of warm and cool,
    as if, beyond the instinctive dread of suffocation
    and darkness, lay a return to something I had known,
a kind of tender vertigo, and I am unable

to decide whether or not I should resist.
    These four-by-fours, of course, would make a fine
        martyrdom,
    but I know that story, and it's different from
this feeling of recovering something lost:

. . .

a bit of faience ware, a buried silver spoon,

a rusted padlock or a toy paratrooper,

his arms folded patiently across his chest since the year

the boy lost him, playing, who has become a man.

IN THE GARDEN (3)

Hydrangea deepens through each litmus color:
a month more and the summer will be gone.
Standing on line at the pharmacy,
I notice the boxed tests of No-Confidence
for cannabis, cocaine, methamphetamines.

CRAPE MYRTLE

Under a tree, my Dying Gaul
(I bought him at a library book sale)
revolves around his mortal wound,

rain-slick, spattered with fallen blossom,
the shield he lies on like a turntable
for some timeless aria of woe

—sung by the bullhead conqueror
whose portrait bust was pulled from the river,
a gloomy world of wrecked cars, attacks

by the mud pout, rotting tires,
and who, having harrowed the ruck of time,
took the liberty of writing VINDEX

in a prose called beautiful, upright, nude:
They resented having their children
kept as hostages, and were convinced

. . .

their Alpine heights would be forever occupied.
I knew his village: it was Octodurus,
put to the torch by Servius Galba.

Those are its shooting rafters of red flame.

LATE FIGS

Now it is time for mulch in its berm,

    for the shawl of burlap held shut with a pin,

the picnic cooler's helmet of Styrofoam,

bandoliered in duct tape like a victim

    or a toppling Mother Courage in the garden.

The autumn rains have swelled the last fruit

    hanging plump on its umbilical stem,

coy amid the key-and-slot

of shadows that continually fondle it,

    splayed open now by gravity at the bottom,

going brown along the petaled edge

    of a jeweled crimson interior,

weeping in a kind of ambrosial drench

under the press of noon's advantage

    with the burning smell of old sugar.

Take one into your mouth: there is,

    after the down against your palate,

the crush of seeds and a pulpiness,

pleasure edged with a sense of trespass
    that anything so late and so sweet

should live in you. Nor is it for long:
    the few remaining on a meandered dish,
plucked from the frost and the blackening
clench of leaves, are freckled by morning
    with a blue mold satiety will not touch.

MILKWEED

And then, after an absence, to return
  with only her, one afternoon in March,
and find, in that place where you once lay down,
  a badge of glittering corn snow. The urge,

the body's absolute hunger for the light . . .
  The log-and-daub's a quarter mile away
where Varnum's men, in their low encampment,
  died of putrid fever and dysentery.

Blown gray pods stand by, avidly listening,
  backlit by sun and glowing like an ear.
A young man splits one still intact, laughing:
  the white seed drifts and streams around his lover.

In this stone farmhouse Varnum held courts-martial,
  in a dark room where soon the westering sun,
angling through a small window, fires a bowl,
  its common earthenware, its lip glazed green.

TWO CARDINALS

i.m. Richard Faxon

It was early spring,

    the landscape dull

with its long perishing,

    reluctant, irreducible,

and by the empty urn,

    the dark blot of the yew,

like a sleeve of crimson

    flame, I saw

a pair of cardinals rise

    into the famished air,

a motion that was

    somehow familiar

in its woven spiral.

    Tall, thin, passion-fed

at the Communion rail,

    his chasuble embroidered

      *   *   *

over a surplice whiter
    than the March snow
of retreating winter
    forty years ago,

who saw my little strength
    and my deficiencies;
who smiled and spoke with
    a voice that was my voice:

I do not want
    your kind of love,
lest it melt my heart
    and I be changed, and live.

And though I shrank from him,
    how eagerly I would
follow now, and climb
    the raw gray air outside.

NOTES

"New Gulph Road"
The italicized passage comes from the *Bhagavad Gita* 7:9, in the translation by Juan Mascaró.

"Wissahickon Schist"
Wissahickon schist is quarried in southeastern Pennsylvania.

"Belfagor"
Belfagor, or Berfagor, is a minor forest deity in northern Italy and Canton Ticino, Switzerland. William-Adolphe Bouguereau (1825–1905) was a French Academic painter.

"Mount Lebanon"
The second American settlement of the celibate utopian community known as the Shakers was on Lebanon Mountain, in Columbia County, New York. One of the Elders was Frederick W. Evans, who is interviewed in Charles Nordhoff's book originally published as *The Communistic Societies of the United States* (1875). In the eighteenth and nineteenth centuries, a popular spa at nearby Lebanon Springs provided a point of departure for tourists wishing to visit the Shakers.

The poem includes phrases from accounts of visits to the settlement.

"Alaric and Romanus"
The story of Alaric is taken from Edward Gibbon's *Decline and Fall of the Roman Empire*, chapter 31. The other story is from Steven Runciman, *The Emperor Romanus Lecapenus and His Reign* (1929), pp. 234–236.

"The Lake"
Aeneas loses his wife, Creusa, during Troy's last night, as narrated in book II of Virgil's *Aeneid*. The lake described is Lac Léman (Lake Geneva), in French Switzerland.

"Propofol"
Propofol is a surgical anesthetic. The Belgian artist Félicien Rops (1833–1898) titled a work of 1878–1879 *Pornokrates*, suggesting the power of harlots.

"ΛΗΜΝΟΣ"
The Greek letters spell "Lemnos," the name of a barren island in the northern Aegean where the Homeric hero and archer Philoctetes (subject of a play by Sophocles) was abandoned because of the putrefaction of his wounded foot, and where the forge god Hephaestus fell to earth when cast down from Mount Olympus.

"Sonnet"
The last two italicized lines of the poem are quoted from David Grene's translation of Euripides' *Hippolytus*.

"July 20, 1969"
The date is that of the first moon landing, by Neil Armstrong
and Buzz Aldrin, who with Michael Collins formed the crew of
Apollo 11.

"Love in the Museum"
The outstanding and idiosyncratic art collection belonging to
Dr. Alfred Barnes, housed for many years in a mansion in
Merion, Pennsylvania, is scheduled to open in a new museum
in downtown Philadelphia in 2012.

"Fine Work with Pitch and Copper"
The title is taken from a poem by William Carlos Williams.

"Viagra Nation"
Pentheus meets his doom at the end of Euripides' last play,
The Bacchae, and also at the end of book III of Ovid's
Metamorphoses.

"After Three Years" (Verlaine)
The "barbarian prophetess" is Veleda, a Germanic priestess who
guided an uprising against Rome under Vespasian (mentioned
by Tacitus); she was a popular figure for garden statues in
nineteenth-century France.

"Gout-Weed"
The plant described is also known as bishop's weed or ground
elder. The work by Johann Sebastian Bach is an Easter cantata,
BWV 4, *Christ Lay in the Thrall of Death.*

"Siberian Iris"
The American landings on Saipan, a Pacific island in the
Northern Marianas, began on June 15, 1944.

"Fireflies"
The first line is from Paul Verlaine's early poem "L'heure du
berger" ("Lovers' Moment"). Ezra Pound's early book of poems
(1908) is titled *A Lume Spento* (*With Tapers Quenched*).

"Epigrams on the Fig"
Hephaestus, the Greek god of the forge, was associated with
Lemnos, possibly because of the island's volcanic activity. The
poem incorporates lines from *Paradise Lost*, from Shakespeare,
and from Virginia Woolf's memoir "A Sketch of the Past."

"In the Garden" (2)
The photograph described, from the Vietnam War, was taken by
Huỳnh Công Út (Nick Ut) in 1972 and received a Pulitzer Prize.
U.S. Army general William Westmoreland reportedly dismissed
it as a fake, saying that the girl depicted had been burned "in a
hibachi accident."

"A Cement Lawn Statue"
The poem is in sapphics.

"Crape Myrtle"
An article in *The New York Times* of November 29, 2009, by
Maïa de la Baume describes the recovery of a portrait bust of
Julius Caesar from the Rhône River at Arles, France. The *Dying*

Gaul is a Roman marble copy of a lost Hellenistic original. The italicized lines in the poem are adapted from S. A. Handford's translation of Caesar's *The Conquest of Gaul*. Octodurus was on the site of modern-day Martigny, in Switzerland.

"Milkweed"
The poem is set in Valley Forge, now a national park, where George Washington's armies passed the grim winter of 1777–1778. James Varnum (1748–1789), who was commissioned Colonel of the First Regiment of Rhode Island in 1775, was encamped there.

ABOUT THE AUTHOR

Karl Kirchwey is the author of five previous books of poems: *A Wandering Island* (1990; recipient of the Norma Farber First Book Award from the Poetry Society of America), *Those I Guard* (1993), *The Engrafted Word* (1998; a *New York Times* Notable Book of the Year), *At the Palace of Jove* (2002), and *The Happiness of This World: Poetry and Prose* (2007). His work has appeared in most of this country's major literary journals; his essays and reviews have been published in *Parnassus: Poetry in Review*, *The Philadelphia Inquirer*, *The New York Times Book Review*, and elsewhere. He is also the author of a verse play, *Airdales & Cipher*, based on the *Alcestis* of Euripides, and his translation of Paul Verlaine's first book, *Poèmes saturniens* (*Poems Under Saturn*), is published by Princeton University Press.

Kirchwey has received grants from the Ingram Merrill and Guggenheim foundations, as well as an NEA literary fellowship and the Rome Prize in Literature. From 1987 to 2000, he was director of the Poetry Center of the 92nd Street YM-YWHA in New York City. He is professor of the arts and director of the Creative Writing Program at Bryn Mawr College, and from 2010 to 2013 is serving as Andrew Heiskell Arts Director at the American Academy in Rome.